## Measure It!

# How Do You Measure Time?

by Thomas K. and
Heather Adamson

**CAPSTONE PRESS**
a capstone imprint

# Yippee!

Vacation is coming in one month.
Ann's family is going on a ski trip.

# How long will one month take?

A month is longer than a week.
But it's shorter than a year.

Blue & gold macaw (Ara ararauna)                                    ©2009 Brian Kenney

## JANUARY 2010
janvier · enero · januar

| SUNDAY | MONDAY | TUESDAY | WEDNESDAY | THURSDAY | FRIDAY | SATURDAY |
|--------|--------|---------|-----------|----------|--------|----------|
| 27 | 28 | 29 | 30 | 31 | 1 | 2 |
| 3 | 4 | 5 | 6 | 7 | 8 | 9 |
| 10 | 11 | 12 | 13 | 14 | 15 | 16 |
| 17 | 18 | 19 | 20 | 21 | 22 | 23 |
| 24 | 25 | 26 | 27 | 28 | 29 | 30 |
| 31 | 1 | 2 | 3 | 4 | 5 | 6 |

Parrots

People around the world measure time the same way. Short bits of time are measured in seconds, minutes, and hours.

Longer amounts of time are measured in days, weeks, months, and years. Ann has many things that measure time in her house.

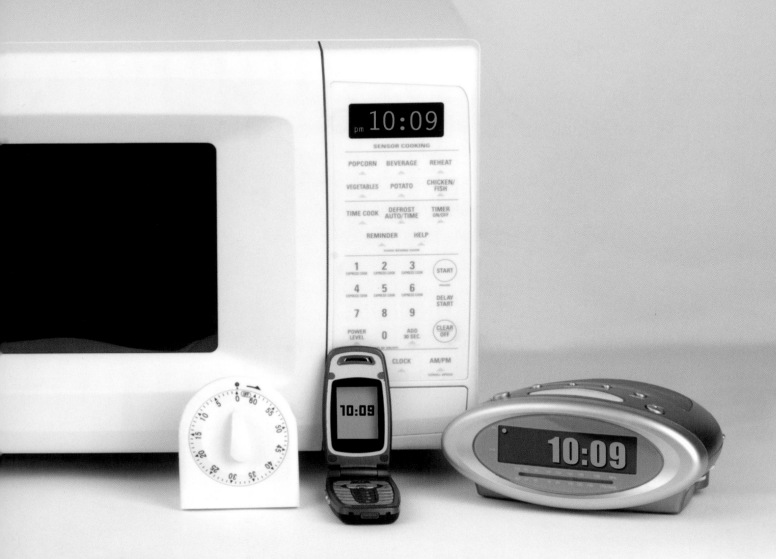

Clocks measure seconds, minutes, and hours. The fast-moving pointer moves every second. It takes 60 seconds to go around the clock. Sixty seconds equals one minute. The minute pointer takes one minute to move to the next mark. The hour pointer takes 60 minutes to move to the next number.

Watches are small clocks.
Ann's dad looks at his watch.
He tells Ann it's time for school.

Calendars keep track of longer amounts of time. Each month gets a page.

## JANUARY

| Sunday | Monday | Tuesday | Wednesday | Thursday | Friday | Saturday |
|---|---|---|---|---|---|---|
|  |  |  |  |  | 1 | 2 |
| 3 | 4 | 5 | 6 | 7 | 8 | 9 |
| 10 | 11 | 12 | 13 | 14 | 15 | 16 |
| 17 | 18 | 19 | 20 | 21 | 22 | 23 |
| 24 31 | 25 | 26 | 27 | 28 | 29 | 30 |

## FEBRUARY

| Sunday | Monday | Tuesday | Wednesday | Thursday | Friday | Saturday |
|---|---|---|---|---|---|---|
|  | 1 | 2 | 3 | 4 | 5 | 6 |
| 7 | 8 | 9 | 10 | 11 | 12 | 13 |
| 14 My Birthday | 15 | 16 | 17 | 18 | 19 | 20 |
| 21 | 22 | 23 Ski Week | 24 | 25 | 26 | 27 |
| 28 |  |  |  |  |  |  |

## MAY

| Sunday | Monday | Tuesday | Wednesday | Thursday | Friday | Saturday |
|---|---|---|---|---|---|---|
|  |  |  |  |  |  | 1 |
| 2 | 3 | 4 | 5 | 6 | 7 | 8 Dance Recital |
| 9 | 10 | 11 | 12 | 13 | 14 | 15 |
| 16 | 17 | 18 | 19 | 20 | 21 | 22 |
| 23 30 | 24 31 | 25 | 26 | 27 | 28 | 29 |

## JUNE

| Sunday | Monday | Tuesday | Wednesday | Thursday | Friday | Satu |
|---|---|---|---|---|---|---|
|  |  | 1 | 2 | 3 | 4 | 5 |
| 6 | 7 | 8 | 9 | 10 | 11 | 12 |
| 13 | 14 | 15 | 16 | 17 | 18 | 19 |
| 20 | 21 | 22 | 23 | 24 | 25 | 26 |
| 27 | 28 | 29 | 30 |  |  |  |

## SEPTEMBER

| Sunday | Monday | Tuesday | Wednesday | Thursday | Friday | Saturday |
|---|---|---|---|---|---|---|
|  |  |  | 1 | 2 | 3 | 4 |
| 5 | 6 | 7 | 8 | 9 | 10 | 11 |
| 12 | 13 | 14 | 15 | 16 | 17 | 18 |
| 19 | 20 | 21 | 22 | 23 | 24 | 25 |
| 26 | 27 Mom's Birthday | 28 | 29 | 30 |  |  |

## OCTOBER

| Sunday | Monday | Tuesday | Wednesday | Thursday | Friday |  |
|---|---|---|---|---|---|---|
|  |  |  |  |  | 1 |  |
| 3 | 4 | 5 | 6 | 7 | 8 |  |
| 10 | 11 | 12 | 13 | 14 | 15 |  |
| 17 | 18 | 19 | 20 | 21 | 22 |  |
| 24 31 | 25 | 26 | 27 | 28 | 29 |  |

## MARCH

| Monday | Tuesday | Wednesday | Thursday | Friday | Saturday |
|---|---|---|---|---|---|
| 1 | 2 First Soccer Practice | 3 | 4 | 5 | 6 |
| 8 | 9 | 10 | 11 | 12 | 13 |
| 15 | 16 | 17 | 18 | 19 | 20 |
| 22 | 23 | 24 | 25 | 26 | 27 |
| 29 Spring Break | 30 | 31 | | | |

## APRIL

| Sunday | Monday | Tuesday | Wednesday | Thursday | Friday | Saturday |
|---|---|---|---|---|---|---|
| | | | | 1 | 2 | 3 |
| 4 | 5 | 6 | 7 | 8 | 9 | 10 |
| 11 | 12 | 13 | 14 | 15 | 16 | 17 |
| 18 | 19 | 20 | 21 | 22 | 23 | 24 |
| 25 | 26 | 27 | 28 | 29 | 30 | |

## JULY

| Monday | Tuesday | Wednesday | Thursday | Friday | Saturday |
|---|---|---|---|---|---|
| | | | 1 | 2 | 3 |
| 5 | 6 | 7 | 8 | 9 Dad's Birthday | 10 |
| 12 | 13 | 14 | 15 | 16 | 17 |
| 19 | 20 | 21 | 22 | 23 | 24 |
| 26 | 27 | 28 | 29 | 30 | 31 |

## AUGUST

| Sunday | Monday | Tuesday | Wednesday | Thursday | Friday | Saturday |
|---|---|---|---|---|---|---|
| 1 | 2 | 3 | 4 | 5 | 6 | 7 |
| | | Camping Week | | | | |
| 8 | 9 | 10 | 11 | 12 | 13 | 14 |
| 15 | 16 | 17 | 18 | 19 | 20 | 21 |
| 22 | 23 | 24 | 25 | 26 | 27 | 28 |
| 29 | 30 | 31 First Day of School | | | | |

## NOVEMBER

| Sunday | Monday | Tuesday | Wednesday | Thursday | Friday | Saturday |
|---|---|---|---|---|---|---|
| | 1 | 2 | 3 | 4 | 5 | 6 |
| | 8 | 9 | 10 | 11 | 12 | 13 |
| | 15 | 16 | 17 | 18 | 19 | 20 |
| 21 | 22 | 23 | 24 | 25 | 26 | 27 |
| 28 | 29 | 30 | | | | |

## DECEMBER

| Sunday | Monday | Tuesday | Wednesday | Thursday | Friday | Saturday |
|---|---|---|---|---|---|---|
| | | | 1 | 2 | 3 | 4 |
| 5 | 6 | 7 | 8 | 9 | 10 | 11 |
| 12 | 13 | 14 | 15 | 16 | 17 | 18 |
| 19 | 20 | 21 | 22 | 23 | 24 | 25 |
| 26 | 27 Winter Break | 28 | 29 | 30 | 31 | |

A calendar shows how many days and weeks are in a month. Ann's big ski trip is next month.

9

It's hard to wait for vacation to come. Ann tests what each amount of time feels like.

How many times can Ann jump rope in one minute? Ann jumps 50 times.

10

A minute feels like a short time when she's jumping rope. But it feels long when she tries to hold her breath.

# An hour is longer than a minute.

Ann's ballet class lasts one hour. All that spinning and jumping is a good workout!

She's glad to rest and watch a movie. A movie lasts about two hours.

# A whole day lasts from midnight to midnight.

A day has 24 hours. Most days, Ann gets up and goes to school. Later, she spends the evening with her family. But today is Saturday. Ann is sleeping in.

| Sunday | Monday | Tuesday | Wednesday | Thursday | Friday | Saturday |
|--------|--------|---------|-----------|----------|--------|----------|
| 21 No School | 22 | 23 | 24 | 25 | 26 | 27 No School |
| | ├── | School | Days | | ──┤ | |

Seven days equals one week. Some things happen once a week. Ann has Spanish class at school each Monday. Family game night is every Friday. Hurry before time runs out!

A month is about four weeks long. Ann and her family go to the library once a month. Ann will find books to read before vacation.

Ann's birthday comes once a year. A year is 12 months long. Last year Ann was 7 years old. Now she is 8. Next year, Ann will be 9 years old.

**FEBRUARY** 2010
février · febrero · februar

| SUNDAY | MONDAY | TUESDAY | WEDNESDAY | THURSDAY | FRIDAY | SATURDAY |
|--------|--------|---------|-----------|----------|--------|----------|
|  | 1 ✕ | 2 ✕ | 3 ✕ | 4 ✕ | 5 ✕ | 6 ✕ |
| 7 ✕ | 8 ✕ | 9 ✕ | 10 ✕ | 11 ✕ | 12 ✕ | 13 ✕ |
| 14 My 8th Birthday | 15 | 16 | 17 | 18 | 19 | 20 |
| 21 | 22 | 23 | 24 | 25 | 26 | 27 |
| 28 | | | | | | |

├———— Ski Week ————┤

**FEBRUARY** 2011
février · febrero · februar

| SUNDAY | MONDAY | TUESDAY | WEDNESDAY | THURSDAY | FRIDAY | SATURDAY |
|--------|--------|---------|-----------|----------|--------|----------|
|  | 1 | 2 | 3 | 4 | 5 |
| 6 | 7 | 8 | 9 | 10 | 11 | 12 |
| 13 | 14 My 9th Birthday | 15 | 16 | 17 | 18 | 19 |
| 20 | 21 | 22 | 23 | 24 | 25 | 26 |
| 27 | 28 | | | | | |

**20**

21

It doesn't take as long as a birthday for vacation to come. It has been a month. Ann finishes her library books.

Ann's family leaves tomorrow!

FEBRUARY 2010

Ski Week

22

# How Do You Measure Time?

September

| SUNDAY | MONDAY | TUESDAY | WEDNESDAY | THURSDAY | FRIDAY | SATURDAY |
|--------|--------|---------|-----------|----------|--------|----------|

by Thomas K. and Heather Adamson

A+ books

23

Vacation time is finally here!
Ann packs her suitcase. Vacation
will last one week.

**That's seven days of fun!**

# Ann's Ski Vacation

There are so many ways to measure time—the seconds they smile for pictures, the minutes they laugh, and the hours they ski.

Only a few vacation days are left. Then Ann will have to wait a whole year until ski trip time comes again.

# Cool Measuring Facts

• Before clocks, people used sundials to tell the time. The sun would shine on the sundial. The shadow the dial created pointed to what time it was.

• It takes 29.5 days to go from one full moon to the next full moon.

• A cheetah can go 100 feet (30 meters) in one second at its top speed.

- Stephen Clarke carved a face into a pumpkin in 24 seconds. That time is a world record.

- How long does it take you to eat a slice of pizza? Josh Anderson ate a whole pizza in one minute, 45 seconds.

- Kiev, Ukraine, has the world's largest floral clock. The clock face is 54 feet (16.5 meters) across and is made of flowers.

# Glossary

**calendar**—a chart showing all the days, weeks, and months in a year

**clock**—a tool that tells time; the hands on a clock point to the hour, minute, and second

**day**—a 24-hour period, from midnight to midnight

**hour**—a unit of time that is equal to 60 minutes

**measure**—to find out the amount of something

**minute**—a unit of time that is equal to 60 seconds

**month**—one of the 12 parts that make up a year

**second**—a very short unit of time

**week**—a period of seven days

**year**—a period of 12 months